THE RUSSIAN REVOLUTION

History SparkNotes

D1153538

Spark Educational Publishing
A Division of Barnes & Noble Publishing
120 Fifth Avenue
New York, NY 10011
www.sparknotes.com

ISBN 1-4114-0430-0

Please submit all comments and questions or report errors to *www.sparknotes.com/errors*.

Printed and bound in the United States.

Contents

Overview

The Russian Revolution took place in 1917, during the final phase of World War I. It removed Russia from the war and brought about the transformation of the Russian Empire into the Union of Soviet Socialist Republics (USSR), replacing Russia's traditional monarchy with the world's first Communist state. The revolution happened in stages through two separate coups, one in February and one in October. The new government, led by Vladimir Lenin, would solidify its power only after three years of civil war, which ended in 1920.

Although the events of the Russian Revolution happened abruptly, the causes may be traced back nearly a century. Prior to the revolution, the Russian monarchy had become progressively weaker and increasingly aware of its own vulnerability (and therefore more reactionary). Nicholas II—the tsar who led Russia in the years leading up to the revolution—had personally witnessed revolutionary terrorists assassinate his grandfather and, subsequently, his own father respond to the assassination through brutal oppression of the Russian people. When Nicholas II himself became tsar in 1894, he used similarly severe measures to subdue resistance movements, which were becoming bolder and more widespread every year. As Nicholas's newly imposed oppressions in turn incited still more unrest, he was forced to make concessions after each incident: it was in this manner that Russia's first constitution was created, as was its first parliament. These concessions continued gradually until Nicholas II's grip on power became very tenuous.

As Nicholas II grew weaker, Vladimir Lenin rose to prominence as the most powerful figure in Russia. Although this famous leader of the October Revolution was not even in Russia for the February Revolution—he had lived in self-imposed exile in Europe since 1900 and returned to Russia only in April 1917—he nonetheless exerted tremendous influence. Whatever history's judgment of him, few other Russian revolutionaries possessed Lenin's decisiveness and strength of vision for Russia's future. Born in 1870 in the provincial town of Simbirsk as Vladimir Ilich Ulyanov, the young Lenin was profoundly affected by his older brother Alexander's 1887 execution for being involved in a plot to assassinate the tsar. As a young adult, Vladimir joined the resistance movement himself and took the pseudonym Lenin but swore that he would never engage in the sort of "adventurism" that had ended his brother's life. Nevertheless, his actions would one day become very adventurous indeed.

The revolution that Lenin led marked one of the most radical turning points in Russia's 1,300-year history: it affected economics, social structure, culture, international relations, industrial development, and most any other benchmark by which one might measure a revolution. Although the new government would prove to be at least as repressive as the one it replaced, the country's new rulers were drawn largely from the intellectual and working classes rather than from the aristocracy—which meant a considerable change in direction for Russia.

The revolution opened the door for Russia to fully enter the industrial age. Prior to 1917, Russia was a mostly agrarian nation that had dabbled in industrial development only to a limited degree. By 1917, Russia's European neighbors had embraced industrialization for more than half a century, making technological advancements such as widespread electrification, which Russia had yet to achieve. After the revolution, new urban-industrial regions appeared quickly in Russia and became increasingly important to the country's development. The population was drawn to the cities in huge numbers. Education also took a major upswing, and illiteracy was almost entirely eradicated.

The Russian Revolution also had considerable international consequences. Lenin's government immediately pulled Russia out of World War I, changing the balance of forces for the remaining participants. During the ensuing civil war in Russia, several nations, including the United States, sent troops to Russia in hopes of keeping the chaos from spreading beyond Russia's boundaries. Over the next several decades, the Soviet Union actively sponsored and assisted Communist movements and revolutions around the world in an effort to broaden its sphere of influence. The country also played a fundamental role in the defeat of Nazi Germany during World War II.

Threatened by the possibility of revolutions in their own lands, the governments of many Western nations viewed Communism as a spreading threat and moved to isolate the Soviet Union as much as possible. Following World War II and the advent of the nuclear age, a confrontation between the Soviet Union and the United States took center stage. As this Cold War got under way, the two countries emerged as superpowers with much of the rest of the world falling in behind one or the other. A protracted nuclear arms race between the United States and Soviet Union would last until the USSR finally collapsed in 1991.

SUMMARY OF EVENTS

THE FEBRUARY REVOLUTION

The Russian Revolution of 1917 centers around two primary events: the February Revolution and the October Revolution. The **February Revolution**, which removed Tsar **Nicholas II** from power, developed spontaneously out of a series of increasingly violent demonstrations and riots on the streets of **Petrograd** (present-day St. Petersburg), during a time when the tsar was away from the capital visiting troops on the World War I front.

Though the February Revolution was a popular uprising, it did not necessarily express the wishes of the majority of the Russian population, as the event was primarily limited to the city of Petrograd. However, most of those who took power after the February Revolution, in the **provisional government** (the temporary government that replaced the tsar) and in the **Petrograd Soviet** (an influential local council representing workers and soldiers in Petrograd), generally favored rule that was at least partially democratic.

THE OCTOBER REVOLUTION

The **October Revolution** (also called the **Bolshevik Revolution**) overturned the interim provisional government and established the **Soviet Union**. The October Revolution was a much more deliberate event, orchestrated by a small group of people. The **Bolsheviks,** who led this coup, prepared their coup in only six months. They were generally viewed as an extremist group and had very little popular support when they began serious efforts in April 1917. By October, the Bolsheviks' popular base was much larger; though still a minority within the country as a whole, they had built up a majority of support within Petrograd and other urban centers.

After October, the Bolsheviks realized that they could not maintain power in an election-based system without sharing power with other parties and compromising their principles. As a result, they formally abandoned the democratic process in January 1918 and declared themselves the representatives of a **dictatorship of the proletariat**. In response, the **Russian Civil War** broke out in the summer of that year and would last well into 1920.

A Note on the Russian Calendar

Until February 1918, Russia used the **Julian calendar**, while the Western world used the **Gregorian calendar** in use today. This convention was dictated by the Russian Orthodox Church, which continues to follow the Julian calendar to this day. During the twentieth century, the Julian calendar fell thirteen days behind the Gregorian calendar. Generally, historians writing about pre-revolutionary Russia today cite dates according to the calendar of the time; this book follows the same method. Dates prior to February 1, 1918 use the Julian calendar; dates after that point follow the Gregorian calendar.

KEY PEOPLE & TERMS

PEOPLE

ALEXANDER I
The Russian **tsar**, or emperor, whose death in 1825 prompted a mild secession crisis that created an appearance of weakness in the Russian monarchy. A group of 3,000 soldiers who termed themselves **Decembrists** took advantage of the chaos to demand reforms, such as a written constitution for Russia. Later revolutionaries such as Lenin saw the Decembrists as heroes.

ALEXANDER II
The Tsar who formally abolished **serfdom** in 1861, freeing Russia's serfs from indentured servitude to their landowners. Though reformers hailed the move, it engendered a severe economic crisis, angered landowners, and prompted a number of revolutionary groups to agitate for a constitution. In 1881, Alexander II was assassinated by a member of one of these groups, prompting his successor, son **Alexander III**, to implement a harsh crackdown on public resistance.

ALEXANDER III
The son of and successor to the assassinated Tsar **Alexander II**. Upon taking power in 1881, Alexander III cracked down severely on reform and revolutionary groups, prompting growing unrest. Alexander III's son, **Nicholas II**, was the tsar in power during the Russian Revolution in 1917.

FELIX DZERZHINSKY
A Polish-born revolutionary who joined the **Bolshevik Party** after getting out of prison in 1917. Following the October Revolution, Vladimir Lenin appointed Dzerzhinsky head of the **Cheka**, the first Soviet secret police force and an early forerunner of the **KGB**.

LEV KAMENEV (A.K.A. LEV ROSENFELD)
A prominent member of the **Bolshevik Party** who initially resisted Lenin's call to hold a revolution sooner rather than later. After the revolution, Kamenev went on to serve in the Soviet government but was executed during **Josef Stalin**'s purges of the 1930s.

ALEXANDER KERENSKY

A member of the Socialist Revolutionary Party and an active participant in both the **provisional government** and the **Petrograd Soviet**. At first, Kerensky acted as a liaison between the two governing bodies. Within the provisional government, he served as minister of justice, minister of war, and later as prime minister. After the October Revolution, Kerensky fled the country and eventually immigrated to the United States, where he taught Russian history at Stanford University.

VLADIMIR LENIN (A.K.A. VLADIMIR ILICH ULYANOV)

The founder of the **Bolshevik Party**, organizer of the **October Revolution**, and the first leader of the Soviet Union. Lenin spent most of the early twentieth century living in exile in Europe (primarily Britain and Switzerland). He was a devout follower of **Marxism** and believed that once a Communist revolution took place in Russia, Communism would spread rapidly around the world. Though not involved in the February Revolution, he returned to Russia in April 1917 and orchestrated the October Revolution that turned Russia into a Communist state.

NICHOLAS I

The younger brother of and successor to Tsar **Alexander I**. This unorthodox succession from older to younger brother caused a small public scandal in 1825 and enabled the **Decembrist Revolt** to take place. Nicholas I was succeeded by his son, **Alexander II**.

NICHOLAS II

The last Russian tsar, who ruled from 1894 until 1917. Nicholas II, who assumed the throne with trepidation upon his father **Alexander III**'s death, was a clumsy and ineffective leader whose avoidance of direct involvement in government caused resentment among the Russian people and resulted in violence in 1905. Nicholas II abdicated on March 2, 1917, as a result of the **February Revolution**. In July 1918, the **Bolsheviks** executed Nicholas along with his wife, **Alexandra**, and their children.

GRIGORY RASPUTIN

A Russian peasant and self-proclaimed mystic who gained significant influence over Tsar **Nicholas II**'s wife, **Alexandra**, in the years immediately prior to the revolutions of 1917. Rasputin's sexual escapades in the Russian capital of **Petrograd** caused scandal, and the Russian people began to believe that the tsar himself was under Rasputin's influence. Aware that Rasputin's presence was damaging Nicholas II's credibility, supporters of the tsar had Rasputin killed in late 1916.

JOSEPH STALIN (A.K.A. JOSEPH DZHUGASHVILI)

A **Bolshevik** leader who became prominent only after Lenin's return to Petrograd in April 1917. Although Stalin was very much a secondary figure during the **October Revolution**, he did gain Lenin's attention as a useful ally, and following the October coup, Lenin gave him a position in the government as **commissar of nationalities**. As Stalin was a member of an ethnic minority—he was from the central Asian region of Georgia, not Russia proper—Lenin felt he would be an effective ambassador of sorts to the many ethnic minorities within the former Russian Empire. After the revolution, Stalin became increasingly powerful and eventually succeeded Lenin as leader of the Soviet Union upon Lenin's death in 1924.

PETR STOLYPIN

The prime minister under Nicholas II. Stolypin was renowned for his heavy crackdown on revolutionaries and dissidents, in which thousands of suspects were given quick martial trials and promptly executed. A hangman's noose was often referred to at the time as a "Stolypin necktie." Stolypin himself was assassinated in 1911 by a revolutionary activist.

LEON TROTSKY (A.K.A. LEON BRONSTEIN)

A Bolshevik leader and one of the most prominent figures of the **October Revolution**. Trotsky, who was in exile abroad during the February Revolution, returned to Russia in May 1917, closely aligned himself with Lenin, and joined the Bolshevik Party during the summer. Trotsky headed the Revolutionary Military Committee, which provided the military muscle for the October Revolution. After the revolution, he was appointed **commissar of foreign affairs** and led Russia's negotiations with Germany and Austria for the armistice and subsequent peace treaty that made possible Russia's exit from World War I.

GRIGORY ZINOVIEV (A.K.A. OSVEL RADOMYSLSKY)

A prominent member of the Bolshevik Party, closely associated with **Lev Kamenev** and a close friend of Lenin during Lenin's years in exile. Initially resisting Lenin's call to hold a revolution sooner rather than later, Zinoviev played virtually no role in the October Revolution and temporarily receded from party activities after the

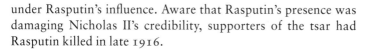

KEY PEOPLE & TERMS

revolution. However, he became a member of the Politburo in 1919 and went on to serve in the Soviet government until he was arrested and executed during Stalin's purges in the 1930s.

TERMS

APRIL THESES
The ideas for Russia's future that **Vladimir Lenin** expressed upon his return to Russia in April 1917. They were published in the newspaper *Pravda* on April 7. In short, Lenin called for the overthrow of the provisional government and its replacement with a communist form of government led by the working class. He believed that other countries would follow Russia's example.

BOLSHEVIKS
A radical political party, led by **Vladimir Lenin,** that split from the **Russian Social Democratic Labor Party** in 1903. The Bolshevik Party favored a closed party consisting of and run by professional revolutionaries and supported the idea of a dictatorship that would accelerate the transition to socialism. It placed an emphasis on the working class, from which it drew much of its support.

CADETS
A political group (an acronym for **Constitutional Democrats**) that wanted to see Russia established as a democratic republic governed by a constitution and an elected parliament. This stance put the Cadets at sharp odds with the **Bolsheviks**, who favored a dictatorship of the proletariat. The Cadets drew support primarily from professional workers and the bourgeois class.

CONSTITUENT ASSEMBLY
An elected body of representatives from around Russia, created in November 1917, that was meant to decide on the country's governmental structure. When **Nicholas II** abdicated in February 1917, the **provisional government** that took power made plans for the formation of this Constituent Assembly in order to choose a more permanent government for Russia. After **Vladimir Lenin** and the **Bolsheviks** took power in the **October Revolution**, they initially allowed elections for the assembly to go forward as scheduled but changed their minds after receiving less than 25 percent of the vote in those elections.

DUAL POWER
A term referring to the two governments that Russia had following the February Revolution—the **provisional government** and the **Petrograd Soviet**.

DUMA
The Russian legislature from 1905–1917. The term, an ancient Russian word referring to small village councils that existed in early Russia, was resurrected when Tsar **Nicholas II** agreed to allow the formation of a legislature after the uprising of 1905. Since the collapse of the Soviet Union in 1991, the term has once more come into use, this time specifically referring to today's lower house of the Russian parliament.

MENSHEVIKS
A political group that, like the **Bolsheviks**, split from the **Russian Social Democratic Labor Party**. The Mensheviks, less radical than the Bolsheviks, supported the idea of a socialistic party that was open to all who wished to join and that would be ruled and organized in a democratic manner.

PETROGRAD SOVIET
A body that existed prior to the February Revolution as a sort of underground revolutionary labor union for workers and soldiers in the Petrograd area, containing members of a number of different political parties. During the February Revolution, members of the Petrograd Soviet saw an opportunity and declared themselves to be the government of Russia. However, they quickly found themselves competing with the **provisional government**.

PROVISIONAL GOVERNMENT
A government that members of the **Duma** formed following the **February Revolution**. The provisional government was meant to be temporary and would rule Russia only until the **Constituent Assembly** decided on a permanent government later.

RUSSIAN SOCIAL DEMOCRATIC LABOR PARTY (RSDLP)
A party that formed in 1898 and was among Russia's earliest revolutionary movements, though by no means the first. In 1903, the RSDLP split into two factions, the **Mensheviks** and the **Bolsheviks**.

SOCIALIST REVOLUTIONARY PARTY (SRs)
A Russian political party during the revolutionary years that was more moderate than the **Bolsheviks** but less so than the **Mensheviks**.

The SRs drew their support primarily from the peasantry and thus had a much larger base than the other parties in Russia. Before and during the **October Revolution**, the SRs were probably the Bolsheviks' closest allies among Russia's many political movements. After the revolution, however, the Bolsheviks abandoned the SRs after the SRs enjoyed a major victory over the Bolsheviks in the elections for the **Constituent Assembly**.

SOVIET

A Russian word literally meaning "council." In the early twentieth century, Soviets were governing bodies, similar to labor unions, that existed primarily on the local/municipal level and collectively made policy decisions for their respective regions. The idea of Soviets was popular among the various socialist parties of the time, including the Bolsheviks, Mensheviks, and Socialist Revolutionaries. When Tsar **Nicholas II** abdicated in early 1917, the powerful **Petrograd Soviet** wielded significant political power in Russia.

SUMMARY & ANALYSIS

A CENTURY OF UNREST

EVENTS

1825	Alexander I dies; succession crisis prompts Decembrist Revolt
1861	Alexander II abolishes serfdom
1881	Alexander II assassinated; Alexander III cracks down on dissenters
1894	Nicholas II becomes tsar
1905	Troops fire on Russian civilians during demonstration in St. Petersburg Russia loses Russo-Japanese War Nicholas II concedes to creation of Russian constitution and Duma
1914	Russia enters World War I

KEY PEOPLE

Alexander I	Tsar whose 1825 death prompted the Decembrist Revolt
Nicholas I	Brother of Alexander I; took power upon Alexander's death
Alexander II	Son of Nicholas I; abolished feudalism in 1861; assassinated in 1881
Alexander III	Son of Alexander II; cracked down harshly on dissenters
Nicholas II	Son of Alexander III; was tsar in power during the 1917 revolutions
Petr Stolypin	Nicholas II's prime minister; had many suspected terrorists tried and executed
Grigory Rasputin	Peasant and mystic who influenced Tsarina Alexandra; was killed by Nicholas II's supporters in 1916

THE DECEMBRIST REVOLT

The first signs of widespread political dissent in Russia surfaced nearly a century before the Russian Revolution, following the death of Tsar **Alexander I** in December 1825. Ever since the **War of 1812**, many Russians, especially military personnel who had served abroad, were inspired by growing democratic movements in Europe. Some even began to call for a formal Russian constitution with guarantees of basic rights. Alexander actually considered the idea of a constitution, and indeed granted one to Poland, but never made up his mind about creating one for Russia.

The tsar's death in 1825 created a fleeting appearance of weakness in the Russian leadership. Alexander had no legitimate children, and there was confusion over which of his two brothers would succeed him. The eldest brother, **Constantine**, was technically next in line but had earlier given up his right to be tsar when he married a woman outside of his class. Therefore, the crown passed to the youngest brother, **Nicholas I**, resulting in a small public scandal. See-ing opportunity in the momentary chaos, 3,000 Russian soldiers marched into the center of St. Petersburg, demanding that Constan-tine take the throne and also calling for a constitution. The uprising was quickly suppressed, and the surviving demonstrators, who called themselves **Decembrists**, were arrested and exiled to Siberia. In the coming years, they came to be seen as heroes among Russian revolutionaries.

EARLY REVOLUTIONARY MOVEMENTS IN RUSSIA

In 1861, Tsar **Alexander II**, Nicholas I's eldest son and successor, formally abolished **serfdom**, freeing Russia's serfs from indenture to landowners. Though a positive development in some ways, it also created a number of new problems, including a severe eco-nomic crisis and significant resentment from landowners. The event also inspired more open discussion of other political reforms, once more raising public awareness of the fact that Rus-sia lacked a constitution.

Throughout the 1860s and 1870s, a host of organizations formed to promote the introduction of a constitution, a parliamen-tary government, and socialistic values to Russia. Although most of these groups were peaceful, some began to toy with the use of vio-lence in order to force change. A series of assassination attempts on Alexander II ensued, and in 1881, one of these attacks succeeded. Members of a group called The People's Will killed Alexander II by throwing a bomb underneath his carriage as it rode through the streets of St. Petersburg. As a result, the new tsar, Alexander's son **Alexander III**, cracked down severely on all forms of public resis-tance. Although the assassination failed to trigger a revolution as the plotters had hoped, the incident did serve as a source of inspira-tion to underground revolutionaries throughout the country, who increasingly saw the autocracy as vulnerable.

RUSSIA AT THE TURN OF THE CENTURY

By the turn of the twentieth century, Russian society had never been more divided, nor had a Russian tsar ever been so far estranged from his people. Tsar **Nicholas II**, who had come to power in 1894, had never shown leadership skills or a particular desire to rule, but with the death of his father, Alexander III, the Russian crown was thrust upon him. In person, Nicholas II was mild-mannered, even meek; lacking the personality of a leader, his rule was clumsy, and he appeared weak before the people. When it came to public opposition or resistance, he avoided direct involvement and simply ordered his security forces to get rid of any problem as they saw fit. This tactic inevitably resulted in heavy-handed measures by the police, which in turn caused greater resentment among the public.

VIOLENCE IN 1905

The year 1905 brought the most extreme examples of Nicholas II's perceived indifference, brutality, and weakness. On Sunday, January 9, a crowd of over 100,000 marched peacefully through the center of St. Petersburg. Eventually they assembled in Palace Square in front of the tsar's Winter Palace and, unaware that the tsar was not in town that day, called for the tsar to appear so that they could present him with a petition.

The police, who had just finished putting down a series of strikes by industrial workers, followed their standing orders to get rid of any problems. Their solution was to open fire on the crowd, which included women and children as well as church leaders. As the crowd scattered, police pursued them on horseback, continuing to fire on them. Many in the crowd were trampled to death in the ensuing panic. Estimates of the total death toll range from a few hundred to several thousand.

News of the massacre spread quickly, and many saw it as a sign that the tsar no longer cared about his people. The incident earned Nicholas the title "Nicholas the Bloody" even though he did not in fact know about the violence until it was already over. An unorganized series of demonstrations, riots, strikes, and assorted episodes of violence erupted across Russia in the following months.

THE RUSSIAN CONSTITUTION AND DUMA

Any chance for Nicholas II to regain his standing was soon lost, as Russia was rocked by a long series of disasters, scandals, and political failures. During the first half of 1905, Russia suffered a humiliating military defeat against Japan. Later in the year, the tsar reluctantly gave in to heavy political pressure and granted Russia its first **constitution**. Permission to form a parliament, called the **Duma**, was also soon granted.

The Duma became a constant thorn in Nicholas's side, as increasingly radical political parties emerged into the open after years of existing underground. Nicholas dealt with the problem by repeatedly dissolving the Duma, forcing new elections. During the same period, a renewed outbreak of assassinations and terrorism prompted the tsar to empower his prime minister, **Petr Stolypin**, to eliminate the threat of terror once and for all. Stolypin established a system of quick military trials for suspected terrorists, promptly followed by public hangings. Thousands were executed over the next several years. In 1911, however, Stolypin himself was fatally shot by an assassin.

RASPUTIN

In the meantime, Nicholas's own family became the subject of a different sort of crisis. His wife, **Alexandra**, had begun consulting with a mystic peasant named **Grigory Rasputin** in a desperate attempt to help her hemophilic son, Alexis. In time, the self-proclaimed monk Rasputin gained political influence over the tsar through his wife, while at the same time engaging in scandalous sexual escapades throughout the Russian capital. Rumors quickly spread that Rasputin had magical powers and that he had the entire royal family under some sort of spell.

WORLD WAR I

It was in the midst of this scandal that Nicholas drew Russia into **World War I** in the summer of 1914. The war was a disaster for Russia: it caused inflation, plunged the country into a food shortage, and ultimately cost the lives of nearly 5 million Russian soldiers and civilians, as well as a series of humiliating military defeats.

The war was the final straw for the Russian people. Although Russian aristocrats had Rasputin killed in a last-ditch effort to preserve the tsar from ruin, it was too late, as popular discontentment was at an all-time high. Within three months, Russia would be without a monarch for the first time in its history.

A COUNTRY RIPE FOR REVOLUTION

In hindsight, nearly a century of warning signs preceded the Russian Revolution, as the Russian aristocracy drifted further and further away from the people over which it ruled. Starting in the early 1700s with Tsar **Peter the Great**, the ruling Romanov family increasingly modeled itself on, and intermarried with, the great royal families of Europe. Over time, the Romanovs estranged themselves from the Russian people and progressively undermined the legitimacy of their own rule.

At the same time, Russians had more exposure to the culture and happenings of Europe than ever before, and many were inspired by the various democratic and socialist movements taking place there. As dissent grew among the Russian people, the monarchy responded with intolerance and by imposing heavy penalties upon all who openly criticized or resisted the government. A series of military failures, starting with the Crimean War in the mid-1800s, and continuing with the Russo-Japanese War of 1904–1905 and finally World War I, further damaged the image of Russia's leaders.

By the early twentieth century, Russia was thus ripe for a revolution. Never in Russian history had so many political organizations existed at the same time. Moreover, many of these organizations were operating outside of Russia itself, where they could plan freely, raise money, and better educate themselves on contemporary political philosophy.

SUMMARY & ANALYSIS

THE FEBRUARY REVOLUTION

EVENTS

February 22, 1917	Nicholas II leaves Petrograd to visit troops
February 23	International Women's Day demonstration in Petrograd
February 24	Massive strikes and demonstrations occur throughout the capital
February 25	Unrest continues; Mensheviks meet and set up a "Workers' Soviet" Nicholas II orders military to stop riots
February 26	Troops fire on demonstrating crowds Mass mutiny begins in local army regiments Firefights break out between troops and police
February 27	More than 80,000 troops mutiny and engage in widespread looting
February 28	Duma and Workers' Soviet gather separately and begin making decisions about restoring order and establishing a new state
March 2	Nicholas II abdicates the throne; provisional government formed

KEY PEOPLE

Nicholas II	Last Russian tsar; abdicated as a result of the February Revolution
Alexander Kerensky	Member of the provisional government and Petrograd Soviet; wielded significant political power after Nicholas II's abdication

INTERNATIONAL WOMEN'S DAY 1917

With Russia faring poorly in **World War I** and facing severe food shortages, strikes and public protests happened in the country with increasing frequency during 1916 and early 1917. Violent encounters between protesters and authorities also increased.

On February 23, 1917, a large gathering of working-class women convened in the center of Petrograd to mark **International Women's Day**. The gathering took the form of a protest demonstration calling for "bread and peace." While the demonstration began peacefully, the next morning it turned violent as the women were joined by hundreds of thousands of male workers who went on strike and flooded the streets, openly calling for an end to the war and even to the monarchy. Feeding on their outrage with each passing day, the demonstrations became larger and rowdier, and the outnumbered police were unable to control the crowds.

VIOLENCE AND ARMY MUTINY

With news of the unrest, Tsar **Nicholas II**, who was away visiting his troops on the front, sent a telegram to Petrograd's military commander on February 25, ordering him to bring an end to the riots by the next day. In their efforts to carry out the tsar's order, several troops of a local guard regiment fired upon the crowds on February

26. The regiment fell into chaos, as many soldiers felt more empathy for the crowds than for the tsar. The next day, more than 80,000 troops mutinied and joined with the crowds, in many cases directly fighting the police.

THE DUMA AND THE PETROGRAD SOVIET

During this period, two political groups in Russia quickly recognized the significance of what was developing and began to discuss actively how it should be handled. The **Duma** (the state legislature) was already in active session but was under orders from the tsar to disband. However, the Duma continued to meet in secret and soon came to the conclusion that the unrest in Russia was unlikely to be brought under control as long as Nicholas II remained in power.

During the same period, the **Petrograd Soviet**, an organization of revolutionary-minded workers and soldiers dominated by the **Menshevik Party**, convened on February 27. They immediately began to call for full-scale revolution and an end to the monarchy altogether.

THE TSAR'S ABDICATION

Despite the mutinies in the army and government, there was still no consensus that the monarchy should be dismantled entirely; rather, many felt that Nicholas II should **abdicate** in favor of his thirteen-year-old son, Alexis. If this occurred, a **regent** would be appointed to rule in the boy's place until he reached maturity. Therefore, both the Duma and military leaders placed heavy pressure on the tsar to resign.

Nicholas II finally gave in on March 2, but to everyone's surprise he abdicated in favor of his brother **Michael** rather than his son, whom he believed was too sickly to bear the burden of being tsar, even with a regent in place. However, on the next day Michael also abdicated, leaving Russia with no tsar at all. Responding to this unexpected turn of events, leading Duma members assumed the role of being the country's **provisional government**. The provisional government was to serve temporarily, until a **Constituent Assembly** could be elected later in the year to decide formally on the country's future government.

THE PROVISIONAL GOVERNMENT AND PETROGRAD SOVIET

Although the provisional government was quickly recognized by countries around the world as the legitimate governing body of Russia, the Petrograd Soviet held at least as much power and had significantly greater connections with regional authorities in other parts of the country. The Petrograd Soviet was in essence a metropolitan labor union made up of soldiers and factory workers. By the time of Nicholas II's abdication, it had some 3,000 members and had formed an executive committee to lead it. Dominated by Mensheviks, the group was chaotic in structure and favored far more radical changes than did the provisional government.

Though often at odds, the provisional government and the Petrograd Soviet found themselves cooperating out of necessity. With every major decision, the two groups coordinated with each other. One man, an ambitious lawyer named **Alexander Kerensky**, ended up a member of both groups and acted as a liaison between them. In time he would become the Russian minister of justice, minister of war, and then prime minister of the provisional government.

ASSESSING THE FEBRUARY REVOLUTION

The February Revolution was largely a spontaneous event. It began in much the same way as had dozens of other mass demonstrations in Russia in previous years and might well have ended in the same manner, if the military had not gotten involved. There was no plan or oversight for the way it happened, and few, if any, dedicated Russian revolutionaries were involved—most, such as Vladimir Lenin, were out of the country. Afterward, many political groups competed for power, but they did so relatively peacefully. The two main groups, the provisional government and the Petrograd Soviet, disagreed completely about the direction that Russia should take, yet they did manage to work with each other. Meanwhile, the various rival political parties also developed cooperative attitudes and worked with one another. The arrival of Lenin in Russia in April 1917, however, immediately changed the situation.

SUMMARY & ANALYSIS

LENIN AND THE BOLSHEVIKS

EVENTS

April 3, 1917	Lenin arrives in Petrograd
April 7	April Theses published in the newspaper *Pravda*
April 21	First Bolshevik demonstrations

KEY PEOPLE

Vladimir Lenin	Revolutionary and intellectual; founded Bolshevik Party; returned to Russia from exile in April 1917 and advocated armed rebellion to establish Communist state

LENIN'S RETURN TO RUSSIA

During the February Revolution, **Vladimir Lenin** had been living in exile in Switzerland. Though historians disagree about specifics, they concur that the government of **Germany** deliberately facilitated Lenin's return to his homeland in the spring of 1917. Without question, the German leadership did so with the intent of destabilizing Russia. The Germans provided Lenin with a guarded train that took him as far as the Baltic coast, from which he traveled by boat to Sweden, then on to Russia by train. There is also evidence that Germany funded the **Bolshevik Party**, though historians disagree over how much money they actually contributed.

Lenin arrived in Petrograd on the evening of April 3, 1917. His arrival was enthusiastically awaited, and a large crowd greeted him and cheered as he stepped off the train. To their surprise, however, Lenin expressed hostility toward most of them, denouncing both the **provisional government** and the **Petrograd Soviet** that had helped to bring about the change of power. Although a limited sense of camaraderie had come about among the various competing parties ever since the February Revolution, Lenin would have nothing to do with this mentality. He considered any who stood outside his own narrow Bolshevik enclave to be his sworn enemies and obstacles to the "natural" flow of history.

THE APRIL THESES

In the days following his arrival, Lenin gave several speeches calling for the overthrow of the provisional government. On April 7, the Bolshevik newspaper ***Pravda*** published the ideas contained in Lenin's speeches, which collectively came to be known as the **April Theses**.

From the moment of his return through late October 1917, Lenin worked for a single goal: to place Russia under Bolshevik control as quickly as possible. The immediate effect of Lenin's attitude, however, was to alienate most other prominent Socialists in the city. Members of the Petrograd Soviet, and even many members of Lenin's own party, wrote Lenin off as an anarchist quack who was too radical to be taken seriously.

"ALL POWER TO THE SOVIETS"

In the meantime, Lenin pulled his closest supporters together and moved on toward the next step of his plan. He defined his movement by the slogan **"All power to the soviets"** as he sought to agitate the masses against the provisional government. In formulating his strategy, Lenin believed that he could orchestrate a new revolution in much the same way that the previous one had happened, by instigating large street demonstrations. Though the soviets were primarily a tool of the **Mensheviks** and were giving Lenin little support at the moment, he believed he could manipulate them for his own purposes.

FAILED EARLY COUP ATTEMPTS

From the moment Lenin returned to Russia, he began to work toward seizing power for the Bolsheviks using every means available. The first attempt took place in late April, during a sharp disagreement between the provisional government and the Petrograd Soviet over the best way to get Russia out of World War I. As frustrated military personnel began to demonstrate in the streets, the Bolsheviks attempted to agitate the troops by demanding the ouster of the provisional government. However, no coup grew out of these demonstrations, and they dissipated without incident.

During the spring and summer, the Bolsheviks would make several more attempts to bring about a second revolution by inciting the masses. Their repeated failures made it clear to Lenin that a repeat performance of the February Revolution was not to be and that a much more organized, top-down approach would be required.

THE BOLSHEVIKS AND THE MILITARY

Lenin recognized that the current Russian leaders' hesitation to pull the country out of **World War I** was a weakness that could be exploited. He knew that after four years of massive losses and humiliating defeats, the army was ready to come home and was on the verge of revolting. While other politicians bickered over negotiating smaller **war reparations**—and even over whether Russia might possibly make **territorial gains** by staying in the war longer—Lenin demanded that Russia **exit the war immediately**, even if it meant heavy reparations and a loss of territory. With this position, Lenin received growing support throughout the Russian armed forces, which would ultimately be key to his seizing power. Thus, he launched an aggressive propaganda campaign directed specifically at the Russian troops still serving on the front.

Lenin's Radicalism

The period following Lenin's return to Russia was a confusing time for Russian **Socialists**, who previously had held Lenin in high esteem and had believed he would unite them upon his return. Indeed, his radical positions caused greater division than ever among Russia's various political groups. Lenin's refusal to compromise backfired on him, however, and in the autumn he would need the support of these groups in order to secure power.

Eventually, Lenin did backtrack temporarily on his earlier extreme positions, with the aim of garnering more support. In particular, he temporarily embraced the **Petrograd Soviet**. Although this effort did have some limited success, it failed to produce the level of support that Lenin had hoped for. Therefore, he decided to concentrate instead on defaming the **provisional government** and also building up connections within the **military** so that after the revolution, he could deal with all his critics by force.

THE SUMMER OF 1917

EVENTS

June 3, 1917	First Congress of Soviets opens in Petrograd
June 9	Bolsheviks call for demonstrations by civilians and soldiers
	Congress of Soviets votes to ban all demonstrations; Bolsheviks desist
June 16	Final Russian offensive of World War I begins
June 30	Petrograd Machine Gun Regiment is ordered to the front
July 3	Bolsheviks plan massive demonstration against the Petrograd Soviet and the provisional government
July 4	Bolsheviks' July Putsch fails; many Bolsheviks are arrested, but Lenin escapes and goes into hiding
August 27	Kerensky dismisses Kornilov and accuses him of treason
	Kornilov calls on his troops to mutiny

KEY PEOPLE

Vladimir Lenin	Bolshevik leader; made numerous attempts to start second revolution during the summer of 1917
Alexander Kerensky	Minister of war and later prime minister of the provisional government; lost credibility during Kornilov affair
Lavr Kornilov	Commander in chief of the Russian army; became embroiled in misunderstanding with Kerensky
Vladimir Lvov	Russian politician who favored military dictatorship; may have instigated Kornilov affair

THE FIRST CONGRESS OF SOVIETS

Throughout the month of June, the **First All-Russia Congress of Soviets** was held in Petrograd. Out of 784 delegates who had a full vote, the **Bolsheviks** numbered 105; though they were a minority, their voice was loud and clear. As the Congress discussed the future of Russia, doubt was expressed as to whether any existing party was actually willing to accept the responsibility of leading the nation. As if on cue, Lenin promptly stood up and announced, "There is such a party!" Laughter was reportedly heard following Lenin's pronouncement, and few took him seriously. To Lenin, however, it was no joke.

BOLSHEVIK-INCITED DEMONSTRATIONS

On June 9, the Bolsheviks made an **open proclamation** calling for civilians and soldiers alike to fill the streets of the capital and to condemn the **provisional government** and demand an immediate end to the war. Though the proclamation called on demonstrators to state their demands "calmly and convincingly, as behooves the strong," the Bolsheviks' true intention, as always, was to sponsor a violent uprising that would topple the government. That evening, the Congress of Soviets, anticipating the potential for violence, prohibited demonstrations for a period of several days. The Bolsheviks gave in and called off the demonstration, realizing that they still lacked adequate support to carry off a revolution.

RUSSIA'S FINAL WAR OFFENSIVE

In June, Minister of War **Alexander Kerensky** ordered the Russian army to undertake a renewed offensive along the Austrian front in **World War I**. Prior to the offensive's start, Kerensky personally toured the front and delivered rousing speeches to the troops. Once under way, the Russian troops made brief progress against the Austrians and even captured several thousand prisoners. Within a few days, however, German reinforcements appeared, and the Russian troops fled in a general panic.

The operation was a complete failure and weakened Kerensky politically. Recognizing another opportunity, Lenin immediately stepped up his efforts to agitate the Russian masses and eagerly waited for the right moment to stage an armed uprising.

THE JULY PUTSCH

On June 30, the **Petrograd Machine Gun Regiment**, one of the largest and most politically volatile military regiments in the city, was ordered to report for duty on the front. Members of the regiment immediately began to protest, and the ever-watchful Bolsheviks lost no time in directing the full strength of their propaganda machine at whipping the soldiers' discontent into a frenzy.

On July 3, Bolshevik leaders decided to try to use the regiment, in combination with their own armed forces and 20,000 sailors from a nearby naval base, to take over the Petrograd Soviet. The Bolsheviks called for an extraordinary meeting of the workers' section of the Soviet, and the next day, July 4, an armed mob began to assemble outside the Tauride Palace, where the Petrograd Soviet had its headquarters.

The mob had little organization, and as rumors circulated that seasoned troops from the front were on the way to Petrograd to put down the demonstrations, fear spread rapidly through the group, and many began to leave. At the same time, the provisional government released documents to the press purporting that the Bolsheviks were treasonously colluding with Germany, which sowed further doubt and confusion among those in the crowd.

By the end of the day, the mob had dissipated, and frontline troops did indeed come into the capital and restore order. Arrest warrants were issued for all of the Bolshevik leaders. Most were caught but were not prosecuted because of resistance by the Petrograd Soviet. Lenin managed to escape to Finland. Kerensky, for his effectiveness in neutralizing the Bolsheviks, was promoted from minister of war to prime minister.

A Setback for the Bolsheviks

The events of June and July proved conclusively to Lenin that he could not carry out a revolution simply by manipulating crowds of demonstrators. The **July Putsch**, as it came to be called, was a disaster for the Bolsheviks on many levels. The failed coup made them appear reckless and incompetent. The accusations of their collusion with Germany further damaged their reputation, especially among the military, and Lenin was unusually ineffective in countering the charges. At the same time, Kerensky and the provisional government received a brief boost in popularity. Worst of all for the Bolsheviks, most of their leadership, including the crucial figure **Leon Trotsky**, were now in jail, and Lenin was once more in hiding, which made communication and planning difficult.

Lavr Kornilov

In July, Prime Minister Kerensky appointed General **Lavr Kornilov** commander in chief of the Russian army. Kornilov, a popular and highly respected figure in the army, reportedly had little interest in politics but had a strong sense of patriotism. However, Kerensky soon began to fear that Kornilov was plotting to set up a military dictatorship. Kornilov had his own doubts about Kerensky as well, and a mutual lack of trust grew quickly between them. Nevertheless, the two leaders managed to work together in a reasonably professional manner for a time.

The Kornilov Affair

This tenuous relationship quickly fell apart, although it is not clear what exactly transpired. According to one account, **Vladimir Lvov**, a former member of the **Duma** and a member of the provisional government, conceived a means to exploit the bad blood between Kerensky and Kornilov. Lvov believed that the only way to save Russia was to install a military dictator and felt that Kornilov fit the bill. Therefore, without telling Kerensky, Lvov paid a visit to Kornilov, presenting himself as Kerensky's representative. In short, Lvov told Kornilov that Kerensky was offering him **dictatorial powers** in Russia if he would accept them. Next, Lvov visited Kerensky, presenting himself as Kornilov's representative, and informed Kerensky that Kornilov demanded **martial law** be established in Petrograd and that all ministers, including Kerensky, give full authority to Kornilov.

Because neither Kerensky nor Kornilov knew each other's intentions, the situation deteriorated rapidly. Kerensky, believing that Kornilov was leading a coup aimed at unseating him, panicked and publicly accused Kornilov of treason. Kornilov, in turn, was dumbfounded and infuriated at this accusation, as he was under the impression that he had been invited to take power. In his panic, Kerensky appealed to the Bolsheviks for help against a military putsch, but in the end, no military coup materialized.

Other historians believe that the so-called **Kornilov affair** involved far less intrigue and merely arose from a series of misunderstandings. Some contend that Kornilov's coup attempt was genuine, while others suspect that Kerensky led Kornilov into a trap. Moreover, although Lvov did indisputably act as a liaison between the two men, it is not entirely clear that he engineered the rift that developed.

REPERCUSSIONS OF THE KORNILOV AFFAIR

In any case, the Kornilov affair weakened Kerensky and provided Lenin with the opportunity he had been waiting for. The incident had two important effects that hastened the downfall of the provisional government. First, it destroyed Kerensky's credibility in the eyes of the military and made him look foolish and unstable to the rest of the country. Second, it strengthened the Bolsheviks, who used the incident very effectively to boost their own platform. It also gave the Bolsheviks an opportunity to greatly increase their store of weapons when the panicked Kerensky asked them to come to his aid. Altogether, the affair finally set the stage for the Bolsheviks to make a real attempt at revolution that autumn.

SUMMARY & ANALYSIS

THE OCTOBER REVOLUTION

EVENTS

August 31, 1917	Bolsheviks achieve majority in the Petrograd Soviet
September 5	Bolsheviks achieve majority in the Moscow Soviet
October 10	Lenin and the Bolshevik Central Committee decide to proceed with revolution
October 23	Provisional government acts to shut down all Bolshevik newspapers
October 24	Provisional government deploys junkers Bolshevik troops begin to take over government buildings in the city
October 25	Kerensky escapes Petrograd Bolsheviks struggle all day long to capture Winter Palace Second Congress of Soviets convenes
October 26	Provisional government is arrested early in the morning Lenin issues Decree on Peace and Decree on Land Congress approves Soviet of the People's Commissars, with all-Bolshevik membership, as new provisional government

KEY PEOPLE

Vladimir Lenin	Bolshevik leader; became leader of Russia after October Revolution; issued Decree on Peace and Decree on Land
Lev Kamenev	Bolshevik leader who resisted Lenin's plans for a prompt revolution
Grigory Zinoviev	Bolshevik leader who sided with Kamenev, voting against revolution
Alexander Kerensky	Prime minister of provisional government; fled Russia during revolution to live in Europe and then the United States

THE RED RESURGENCE

During late August and September, the Bolsheviks enjoyed a sudden growth in strength, following their failures during the summer. On August 31, they finally achieved a majority in the **Petrograd Soviet**, and on September 5, they won a similar victory in the **Moscow Soviet**. Lenin, fearing arrest after the events of July, continued to hide in rural areas near the Finnish border. As time went on, he become more and more impatient and began calling urgently for the ouster of the provisional government.

Although Prime Minister **Alexander Kerensky**'s authority was faltering, the provisional government was coming closer to organizing the **Constituent Assembly**, which would formally establish a republican government in Russia. Elections for the assembly were scheduled for November 12. Lenin knew that once this process started, it would be far more difficult to seize power while still preserving the appearance of legitimacy. If there were to be another revolution, it had to take place before then.

INTERNAL OPPOSITION

Before a revolution could happen, Lenin faced considerable opposition from within his own party. Many still felt that the timing was wrong and that Lenin had made no serious plans for how the country would be administered after power was seized. On October 10, shortly following Lenin's return to Petrograd, the Bolshevik Party leadership (the **Central Committee**) held a fateful meeting. Few details of this meeting have survived, but it is known that Lenin delivered an impassioned speech in which he restated his reasons for staging the uprising sooner rather than later. Most of those present—only twelve men in all—initially were reluctant. Nevertheless, by the end of the meeting, Lenin had talked all but two of them into approving an armed uprising to oust the provisional government. What had yet to be decided was precisely when the revolution would happen.

FINAL PLANS

During the next two weeks, Lenin's followers remained holed up in their headquarters at the Smolny Institute, a former school for girls in the center of Petrograd, where they made their final plans and assembled their forces. A **Second Congress of Soviets** was now in the works, scheduled for October 25, and the Bolsheviks were confident that they would have its overwhelming support, since they had taken pains to invite only those delegates likely to sympathize with their cause.

Just to be sure, however, the Bolsheviks decided to hold the revolution on the day before the meeting and then to ask the Congress to approve their action after the fact. The two Bolshevik leaders who had voted against the uprising after the October 10 meeting, **Lev Kamenev** and **Grigory Zinoviev**, continued to protest the plan and resist Lenin's preparations. However, at the last moment, they suddenly reversed their position so as not to be left out.

By this point, the Bolsheviks had an army of sorts, under the auspices of the **Military Revolutionary Committee**, technically an organ of the Petrograd Soviet. Lenin and the other Bolshevik leaders, however, knew that these troops were unreliable and had a tendency to flee as soon as anyone fired at them. However, they expected that at least the main Petrograd garrison would support them once they saw that the Bolsheviks had the upper hand.

THE PROVISIONAL GOVERNMENT'S RESPONSE

Although the details may have been secret, by late October it was well known throughout Petrograd that the Bolsheviks were planning something major. Prime Minister Kerensky and other members of the provisional government discussed the matter endlessly; Kerensky pressed for greater security and for the arrest of every Bolshevik who could be found, especially those in the Military Revolutionary Committee. The other ministers resisted Kerensky's suggestions and believed that everything could ultimately be solved by negotiation.

Nonetheless, the provisional government did make a few modest preparatory arrangements. First, it closed down all Bolshevik **newspapers** on October 23. Although this move did actually catch the Bolsheviks off guard, it had little practical effect. Then, on the morning of October 24, the day the uprising was to begin, the provisional government installed **junkers**—cadets from local military academies—to guard government buildings and strategic points around the city. One of these positions was the tsar's old Winter Palace, which the provisional government now used for its headquarters. Places of business closed early that day, and most people scurried home and stayed off the streets.

OCTOBER 24

In truth, little happened on **October 24**, the first day of the Russian Revolution. The main event was that Lenin made his way across town to the Smolny Institute, disguised as a drunk with a toothache. Late that evening, Bolshevik troops made their way to preassigned positions and systematically occupied crucial points in the capital, including the main telephone and telegraph offices, banks, railroad stations, post offices, and most major bridges. Not a single shot was fired, as the junkers assigned to guard these sites either fled or were disarmed without incident. Even the headquarters of the General Staff—the army headquarters—was taken without resistance.

THE SIEGE OF THE WINTER PALACE

By the morning of October 25, the **Winter Palace** was the only government building that had not yet been taken. At 9:00 A.M., Kerensky sped out of the city in a car commandeered from the U.S. embassy. The other ministers remained in the palace, hoping that Kerensky would return with loyal soldiers from the front. Meanwhile, Bolshevik forces brought a warship, the cruiser *Aurora*, up the Neva River and took up a position near the palace. Other Bolshevik forces occupied the Fortress of Peter and Paul on the opposite bank of the river from the palace. By that afternoon, the palace was completely surrounded and defended only by the junker guards inside. The provisional government ministers hid in a small dining room on the second floor, awaiting Kerensky's return.

The Bolsheviks spent the entire afternoon and most of the evening attempting to take control of the Winter Palace and arrest the ministers within it. Although the palace was defended weakly by the junker cadets, most of the Bolshevik soldiers were unwilling to fire on fellow Russians or on the buildings of the Russian capital. Instead, small groups broke through the palace windows and negotiated with the junkers, eventually convincing many of them to give up. Although some accounts claim that a few shots were fired, little or no violence ensued. The ministers were finally arrested shortly after 2:00 A.M. on October 26 and escorted to prison cells in the Peter and Paul Fortress. Kerensky never returned and eventually escaped abroad, living out his life first in continental Europe and then as a history professor in the United States.

THE SECOND CONGRESS OF SOVIETS

Although Lenin had hoped that the revolution would be over in time to make a spectacular announcement at the start of the **Second All-Russia Congress of Soviets** in the late afternoon of October 25, events transpired differently. The Congress delegates were forced to wait for several hours as Bolshevik forces tried to remove the provisional government from the Winter Palace. Lenin became increasingly agitated and embarrassed by the delay. Late in the evening, the Congress was declared open, even though the Winter Palace had still not been taken. Furthermore, despite the Bolshevik leaders' efforts, dedicated Bolsheviks constituted only about half of the 650 delegates at the Congress. Lively debate and disagreement took place both about the Bolshevik-led coup and also about who should now lead Russia. The meeting lasted the rest of the night, adjourning after 5:00 A.M. on October 26.

The Congress resumed once more late the next evening, and several important decisions were made during this session. The first motion approved was Lenin's **Decree on Peace**, which declared Russia's wish for World War I to end but did not go so far as to declare a cease-fire. The next matter to be passed was the **Decree on Land**, which officially socialized all land in the country for redistribution to peasant communes. Finally, a new provisional government was formed to replace the old one until the Constituent Assembly met in November as scheduled. The new government was called the **Soviet of the People's Commissars (SPC)**.

Lenin was its chairman, and all of its members were Bolsheviks. As defined by the Congress, the SPC had to answer to a newly elected Executive Committee, chaired by Lev Kamenev, which in turn would answer to the Constituent Assembly.

LIFE AFTER THE REVOLUTION

Life in Russia after October 25, 1917, changed very little at first. There was no widespread panic among the upper classes, and the people of Petrograd were generally indifferent. Few expected the new government to last for long, and few understood what it would mean if it did. In Moscow, there was a power struggle that lasted for nearly a week. In other regions, local politicians (of various party loyalties) simply took power for themselves. In the countryside, anarchy ruled for a time, and peasants boldly seized land as they pleased, with little interference from anyone. The new Bolshevik-led government, meanwhile, improvised policy quite literally on the fly, with no long-term plan or structure in place other than vague intentions.

ASSESSING THE OCTOBER REVOLUTION

Although the Soviet government went to great lengths for decades to make the "Great October Socialist Revolution" appear colorful and heroic, it was in many ways a mundane and anticlimactic event. There was little if any bloodshed, the provisional government barely tried to resist, and afterward, few Russians seemed to care about or even notice the change in governments. However, this very indifference on the part of the Russian people enabled the new leadership to extend its power quite far, and the October Revolution would soon prove to be a cataclysmic event once its earthshaking effect on Russia and the rest of the world became clear. However bloodless the Russian Revolution initially may have been, it would ultimately cost tens of millions of Russian lives and shock the nation so deeply that it has not yet come to terms with what happened.

As far as historians have been able to determine, Lenin and most of the other major revolutionary figures at his side believed sincerely in their cause and were not motivated purely by a thirst for power. In all likelihood, they seized power believing that they were doing so for the greater good. Ironically, their faith in the socioeconomic models of Marx was on the level of an extreme religious devotion— the very same blind devotion that they often denounced in others. Unfortunately, this steadfast belief in Marxism would come to be implemented through brutal and repressive means.

THE AFTERMATH

EVENTS

November 1917	Nationwide elections for the Constituent Assembly held throughout the month
December 15	Russia signs armistice with the Central Powers
December 20	Cheka established with Dzerzhinsky as its leader
January 5, 1918	Constituent Assembly meets for first and last time
March 3	Russia and Germany sign peace treaty at Brest-Litovsk
May	Bolsheviks institute military conscription
June–July	Russian Civil War begins
August 30	Lenin shot in assassination attempt but survives
September 5	Red Terror begins

KEY PEOPLE

Vladimir Lenin	Leader of Russia after the October Revolution; suppressed dissent by disbanding Constituent Assembly, declaring opposing political parties illegal
Felix Dzerzhinsky	Polish revolutionary whom Lenin appointed head of Cheka secret police
Joseph Stalin	Commissar of nationalities in Lenin's government; succeeded Lenin as leader of Russia in 1924

AN END TO THE WAR

After Lenin's government secured power, one of its first major goals was to get Russia out of **World War I**. Following his Decree on Peace, Lenin sent out diplomatic notes to all participants in the war, calling for everyone to cease hostilities immediately if they did not want Russia to seek a separate peace. The effort was ignored. Therefore, in November 1917, the new government ordered Russian troops to cease all hostilities on the front. On December 15, Russia signed an **armistice** with Germany and Austria, pending a formal peace treaty (the treaty was not completed until March 1918).

Russia's exit from the war was very costly, but Lenin was desperate to end the war at any cost, as the Germans were threatening to invade Petrograd. In the peace, Lenin consented to give up most of Russia's territorial gains since the time of Peter the Great. The lost territories included Finland, Poland, Latvia, Lithuania, Estonia, Ukraine, Belarus, Bessarabia, and the Caucasus region, along with some of the coal-mining lands of southern Russia. The Soviets would not regain these territories until the end of World War II.

SUMMARY & ANALYSIS

THE SPC AND THE NOVEMBER ELECTIONS

Following the revolution and the Second Congress of Soviets, Lenin's new government, the SPC, faced the overwhelming task of governing a country in chaos. Communication was poor, and large chunks of the country, including the Ukraine, were still occupied by foreign armies. Outside of Petrograd and Moscow, especially in more distant regions such as Siberia and Central Asia, it was hard even to define what was happening politically, much less to take control of it.

At least in theory, the SPC was a democratic institution. They had been voted into power (after they had taken it) and were supposed to answer to the Executive Committee and in turn to the future **Constituent Assembly**. Indeed, Lenin, expecting the Bolsheviks to do well, allowed **elections** for members of the Constituent Assembly to proceed as scheduled throughout the month of November. When the final tally was in, however, Bolshevik candidates received less than 25 percent of the vote. The highest percentage, 40 percent, went to the **Socialist Revolutionary (SR)** party, which at the time was mildly sympathetic to the Bolsheviks. However, members of other more hostile parties, including the **Cadets** (Constitutional Democrats), had strong showings as well.

REVOLUTIONARY DICTATORSHIP

Because the Bolsheviks placed only modestly in the elections, the Constituent Assembly became a problem for them. Initially, it appeared that the Bolsheviks might have to make some severe compromises in order to stay in power. However, they dealt with this problem first by declaring the Cadet Party illegal and then by demanding that the Constituent Assembly voluntarily give up its legislative authority—a move that would have remade the body into essentially a rubber stamp for Bolshevik policy.

In the end, the Constituent Assembly met only once, on January 5, 1918. During the meeting, the assembly refused to give up its authority but did nothing to challenge the Bolsheviks, who watched over the meeting with loaded guns. When the assembly adjourned the next morning, the Bolsheviks declared the assembly permanently dissolved and accused its members of being "slaves to the American dollar."

THE THIRD CONGRESS OF SOVIETS

The assembly was replaced by the **Third Congress of Soviets**, 94 percent of whose members were required to be Bolshevik and

SR delegates. The new group quickly ratified a motion that the term "provisional" be removed from the official description of the SPC, making Lenin and the Bolsheviks the permanent rulers of the country.

Until this point, the Bolsheviks had often used word *democracy* in a positive sense, but this changed almost instantly. The Bolsheviks began to categorize their critics as *counterrevolutionaries* and treated them as traitors. The terms *revolutionary dictatorship* and *dictatorship of the proletariat* began to pop up frequently in Lenin's speeches, which began to characterize democracy as an illusionary concept propagated by Western capitalists.

THE BOLSHEVIKS' CONSOLIDATION OF POWER

In March 1918, even as Lenin's representatives were signing the final treaty taking Russia out of World War I, the Bolsheviks were in the process of moving their seat of power from Petrograd to **Moscow**. This largely symbolic step was a part of the Bolshevik effort to consolidate power.

Although symbolism of this sort was a major part of the Bolsheviks' strategy, they knew they also needed military power to force the rest of the country to comply with their vision while discouraging potential foreign invaders from interfering. Therefore, they rebuilt their military force, which now largely consisted of 35,000 Latvian riflemen who had sided with the Bolsheviks when they vowed to remove Russia from World War I. The Latvian soldiers were better trained and more disciplined than the Russian forces upon which the Bolshevik forces had previously relied. These troops effectively suppressed insurrections throughout Russia during the course of 1918 and formed the early core of the newly established **Red Army**.

The other major instrument of Bolshevik power was the secret police, known by the Russian acronym **Cheka** (for Extraordinary Commission to Combat Counterrevolution and Sabotage). Officially formed on December 20, 1917, the Cheka was charged with enforcing compliance with Bolshevik rule. At its command, Lenin placed a Polish revolutionary named **Felix Dzerzhinsky**, who would soon become notorious for the deadly work of his organization. Tens of thousands of people would be murdered at Dzerzhinsky's behest during the coming years.

THE ROOTS OF CIVIL WAR

Although the **Russian Civil War** is a separate topic and not dealt with directly in this text, some introduction is appropriate because the war evolved directly from the circumstances of the Russian Revolution. No specific date can be set forth for the beginning of the war, but it generally began during the summer of 1918. As the Bolsheviks (often termed the **Reds**) were consolidating power, Lenin's opponents were also organizing from multiple directions. Groups opposing the Bolsheviks ranged from monarchists to democrats to militant Cossacks to moderate socialists. These highly divergent groups gradually united and came to fight together as the **Whites**. A smaller group, known as the **Greens**, was made up of anarchists and opposed both the Whites and the Reds.

In the meantime, a contingent of about half a million Czech and Slovak soldiers, taken prisoner by the Russian army during World War I, began to rebel against the Bolsheviks, who were attempting to force them to serve in the Red Army. The soldiers seized a portion of the Trans-Siberian Railway and attempted to make their way across Siberia to Russia's Pacific coast in order to escape Russia by boat. In the course of their rebellion, they temporarily joined with White forces in the central Volga region, presenting the fledgling Red Army with a major military challenge. In response to these growing threats, the Bolsheviks instituted military **conscription** in May 1918 in order to bolster their forces.

THE RED TERROR

At the end of the summer, on August 30, there was an **assassination attempt** on Lenin. He survived, but a brutal crackdown on all forms of opposition commenced shortly thereafter. The Bolsheviks called it the **Red Terror**, and it fully lived up to its name. This was the atmosphere under which the Russian Civil War began. It lasted well into 1920–1921, by which point the Bolsheviks had fully crushed the rebellion.

ASSESSING BOLSHEVIK RUSSIA

After the October Revolution, the Bolsheviks had very little planning in place, and their rule got off to a rough start when they came in behind the SRs in the elections of the Constituent Assembly. The working class was still a minority in Russia; the Bolsheviks would change that in time, but at the outset their rule could be maintained only by force.

The Bolsheviks faced major opposition from within Russia and for many different reasons. Among the most contentious issues was Russia's costly exit from World War I. Though many had wanted out of the war, they did not approve of Lenin's readiness to lose vast amounts of territory. In addition, the Bolsheviks' sudden dismissal of the Constituent Assembly and their silencing of all other political voices was offensive to many as well. The result was the Russian civil war, which would be horrifically painful for the country and that, in the end, would cost even more lives than had World War I. The years following, with the violence of **Joseph Stalin**'s purges and forced collectivization of Russia's lands, would not be much better.

STUDY QUESTIONS & ESSAY TOPICS

Always use specific historical examples to support your arguments.

STUDY QUESTIONS

1. *Compare and contrast the February and October Revolutions.*

The February Revolution grew from a street demonstration gone out of control; there was no single political force behind it, and it was not a strategically planned event. Once the military mutinied and the situation had become uncontrollable, the Duma recognized that the tsar's abdication was the only likely way to quell the unrest. The Duma was Russia's officially sanctioned parliament, and while it certainly had conflicts with the tsar on many issues, it did not have an agenda to remove him from power, nor was it intent on ending the monarchy. When the Duma requested the tsar's abdication, they wanted him to do so only in order to enable his son to take the throne in his stead.

The October Revolution, on the other hand, was a planned coup, designed and brought about by Lenin and the Bolshevik Party. This second revolution was a deliberate attempt to overthrow the current Russian government, seize power, and institute a Communist state in place of the monarchy. While the Bolsheviks did not have a detailed plan for how the new government should be run, they unarguably had a clear vision for what they wanted it to achieve.

2. *Compare the collapse of the Russian monarchy with the collapse of the provisional government. Did the two governments fall apart for the same reasons or for fundamentally different reasons?*

The collapse of the Russian monarchy and the collapse of the provisional government were unrelated, but each marked the downfall of an ineffective government that was perceived as weak or incompetent. Tsar Nicholas II had long been seen as out of touch and ineffective, and Russia's embarrassing and costly military failures in the Russo-Japanese War and World War I reinforced this bad reputation. Although the tsar did have a considerable amount of raw power in his military and secret police forces, these forces were effective only insofar as they were loyal. During the February Revolution, the military, when summoned, failed to follow orders and in fact ended up fighting the police. Without the military, the tsar was unable to hold on to power, and even his own government was helpless to save him.

The provisional government was arguably even weaker than the tsar had been, for it never gained a reliable control over the military, nor did it demonstrate a clear vision for the future. Only the prime minister, Alexander Kerensky, demonstrated determined leadership, but incidents such as the Kornilov affair of August 1917 gave Kerensky and his government an air of incompetence. Moreover, the very nature of the provisional government was temporary, simply something intended to hold Russia together until the Constituent Assembly could be elected and establish a permanent government. This intrinsic flimsiness put the members of the provisional government in an awkward and vulnerable position. Lenin and the Bolsheviks were keenly aware of this vulnerability and timed their October Revolution to take advantage of it.

3. *Bolshevism was a rather extreme political movement and did not have widespread popular support. Discuss the reasons why the October Revolution nonetheless succeeded and why it faced so little serious opposition.*

In some respects, the Bolsheviks' success in the October Revolution seems surprising. The party advocated much more radical policies than their political opponents in Russia at the time, and it is clear that the majority of the Russian population did not share the Bolsheviks' views either. Moreover, Kerensky and the provisional government knew for several weeks that Lenin was planning a major action and did their best to prepare for it. However, despite these factors, the significant leadership vacuum in Russia in October 1917, combined with the Bolsheviks' vagueness about their political goals, enabled them to take control of the country handily.

The political situation in Russia in the fall of 1917 was uncertain at best. The country was in a weak and confused state, reeling from World War I losses and under the vague, ineffective leadership of a

QUESTIONS & ESSAYS

temporary provisional government. Although many in the country were dissatisfied with the provisional government, there was a distinct lack of initiative or willingness to take on the responsibility of leadership. In many respects, Lenin was the only Russian politician at the time who appeared confident and to know what he was doing. Nonetheless, few members of the provisional government, aside from Kerensky, recognized the threat that the Bolsheviks presented. As a result, despite Kerensky's efforts to institute measures against the Bolsheviks, other ministers in the government refused, wanting to pursue negotiations with the Bolsheviks instead.

Adding to the confusion was the fact that the Bolsheviks were somewhat ambiguous about their ultimate goals. Russian leaders indisputably saw Lenin as an extremist, but many dismissed him because they were unaware just how extreme he really was. Moreover, because the various political parties in Russia had cooperated actively with one another and shared power in relatively democratic fashion ever since the February Revolution, many Russian leaders assumed that this measured power-sharing would continue. After the October Revolution, the Bolsheviks allowed this illusion to persist until it became inconvenient, at which point they disbanded the Constituent Assembly and began to rule Russia with an iron fist.

SUGGESTED ESSAY TOPICS

1. *How did the Bolsheviks differ from more moderate socialist groups like the SRs and the Mensheviks?*

2. *Explain the Bolsheviks' German connection and the ways in which it affected them politically.*

3. *Discuss the decline of the Romanov dynasty over the century preceding the revolutions of 1917. What were the sources of discontent with the monarchy, and what events weakened it over time?*

4. *Trace the events of the summer of 1917 and the struggles among the political forces at the time. Consider the effects of events including the First Congress of Soviets, the June offensive, the July Putsch, and the Kornilov affair. How did each of these events affect each side?*

5. *Consider the role of the Russian military in the February and October revolutions as well as in the events in between. How did the military's loyalty shift over time? How did the various sides attempt to gain its loyalty?*

REVIEW & RESOURCES

QUIZ

1. During what international war did the Russian Revolution take place?

    A. World War II
    B. Russo-Japanese War
    C. Napoleonic War
    D. World War I

2. What calendar did Russia use until February 1918?

    A. Julian
    B. Gregorian
    C. Old Slavonic
    D. Hebrew

3. Which tsar did terrorists assassinate in 1881?

    A. Nicholas I
    B. Alexander I
    C. Alexander II
    D. Alexander III

4. What slogan was shouted during the February Revolution?

    A. "Let them eat cake!"
    B. "Freedom and justice!"
    C. "No more war!"
    D. "Bread and peace!"

5. The February Revolution began as a(n)

    A. International Women's Day march
    B. Railroad strike
    C. Food drive for soldiers on the front
    D. Bolshevik rally

6. Where was the tsar during the February Revolution?

    A. Visiting soldiers on the front
    B. In the Winter Palace
    C. At a peace conference in Europe
    D. In the Kremlin

7. As a result of the February Revolution, the tsar

    A. Was thrown out of office
    B. Exiled
    C. Voluntarily abdicated
    D. Was immediately executed

8. After the February Revolution, how many organizations claimed to be the new Russian government?

    A. One
    B. Two
    C. Three
    D. Four

9. The provisional government was made up of

    A. Former members of the Synod
    B. Former ministers under the tsar
    C. Revolutionaries
    D. Former members of the Duma

10. Which country's government aided Lenin in returning to Russia?

    A. France
    B. Germany
    C. Turkey
    D. Britain

11. Upon his return to Russia, how did Lenin view revolutionaries outside his own party?

    A. As friends and allies
    B. As potential Bolsheviks whom he needed to convert
    C. He ignored them
    D. As enemies who might be used temporarily but had to be eliminated in the end

12. What slogan did Lenin use following his arrival in Russia in April 1917?

    A. "There is such a party!"
    B. "All power to the Soviets!"
    C. "Proletarians of the world unite!"
    D. "Onward to the shining future!"

13. What was the set of ideas that Lenin expressed in the newspaper *Pravda* following his return to Russia?

    A. The April Theses
    B. The Communist Manifesto
    C. The Federalist Papers
    D. Das Kapital

14. During the summer following the February Revolution, what did Lenin initially believe was the best strategy for starting a second revolution?

    A. Use loyal troops to attack government buildings
    B. Take control of the press
    C. Encourage mass street riots
    D. Execute the tsar in public

15. The Bolshevik Party drew its support primarily from

    A. Peasants
    B. Aristocrats
    C. The intelligentsia
    D. The working class

16. The Petrograd Soviet was a(n)

    A. Union of workers and soldiers
    B. Organization of ex-monarchists
    C. Society of farmers
    D. Group consisting primarily of lawyers

17. Which of the following events seriously weakened the Bolsheviks?

    A. The First Congress of Soviets
    B. Kerensky's June offensive
    C. The July Putsch
    D. Rasputin's murder

18. Which of the following seriously weakened the provisional government?

    A. The July Putsch
    B. The Kornilov Affair
    C. Elections for the Constituent Assembly
    D. The First Congress of Soviets

19. Who was Lavr Kornilov?

    A. A Bolshevik
    B. A rebellious Cossack
    C. A monarchist army general
    D. Leader of the Petrograd Soviet

20. What happened as a result of the July Putsch?

    A. The provisional government was unseated
    B. The Petrograd Soviet split apart
    C. The army mutinied
    D. Several prominent Bolsheviks were arrested

21. Which is true of the Bolsheviks during August and September 1917?

    A. They split into two factions
    B. They had a strong boost in popular support
    C. They sought monetary assistance from Britain
    D. Lenin was betrayed by Trotsky

REVIEW & RESOURCES

22. In early October 1917 all of the following were true of the Bolsheviks *except*

    A. Many were still uneasy about going ahead with a coup
    B. They held public debates together with members of the provisional government
    C. The Bolsheviks' Central Committee met and decided to overthrow the provisional government
    D. They used the Smolny Institute as a headquarters

23. Which two Bolsheviks were most strongly against starting the revolution sooner rather than later?

    A. Kamenev and Zinoviev
    B. Trotsky and Dzerzhinsky
    C. Stalin and Lunacharsky
    D. Kerensky and Kornilov

24. Which action did the provisional government take against the Bolsheviks just prior to the October Revolution?

    A. Brought in loyal troops from the front
    B. Closed down Bolshevik newspapers
    C. Ordered police to raid the Smolny Institute
    D. Set up barricades around the Winter Palace

25. Who were the "junkers"?

    A. German army officers
    B. Workers in the Petrograd junkyard
    C. Russian army cadets assigned to defend government buildings
    D. Bolshevik military units

26. What was the *Aurora*?

   A. A Russian battleship brought into Petrograd to defend the provisional government
   B. A German yacht on which the peace treaty was signed between Germany and Russia
   C. The first Russian aircraft carrier, brought into service at the end of World War I
   D. A Russian cruiser brought into Petrograd by sailors loyal to the Bolsheviks

27. Why did it take an entire day for the Bolsheviks to capture the Winter Palace?

   A. Neither side was eager to fire on the other, so they negotiated for hours
   B. The palace was heavily guarded, and it took a long time to overcome all resistance
   C. The palace has hundreds of rooms, and it took the Bolsheviks a long time to find where the provisional government was hiding
   D. Lenin hesitated to give the order for his troops to enter the building

28. During the February Revolution, what sparked the mutiny among the soldiers?

   A. Some of the troops were disseminating Bolshevik propaganda within the ranks
   B. The soldiers did not have enough food to eat
   C. The troops were revolted by the idea of firing upon fellow Russians
   D. They were paid off by German spies

29. After the October Revolution, what was Lenin's first official act?

   A. The Decree on Land
   B. The Decree on Property
   C. The Decree on Work
   D. The Decree on Peace

30. What happened to Kerensky after the revolution?

    A. He was imprisoned
    B. He was executed
    C. He fled the country
    D. He joined the Bolsheviks

31. What representative body was meeting in Petrograd on the same day as the October Revolution?

    A. The Constituent Assembly
    B. The Duma
    C. The Central Committee
    D. The Congress of Soviets

32. What was the official name of Lenin's new government?

    A. The Politburo
    B. The Soviet of the People's Commissars
    C. The Executive Committee
    D. The Supreme Soviet

33. Which former critic of Lenin chaired the Executive Committee?

    A. Zinoviev
    B. Trotsky
    C. Dzerzhinsky
    D. Kamenev

34. What was the immediate reaction of Russian upper classes to the October Revolution?

    A. The paid little attention to it
    B. They panicked and fled the country en masse
    C. They started a civil war
    D. They appealed to Britain and the United States for help

35. What was the Bolsheviks' initial policy regarding the Constituent Assembly?

    A.   They cancelled the elections
    B.   They let the elections take place without interference
    C.   They let the elections take place but attempted to manipulate the results
    D.   They let the elections take place but required that 90 percent of the seats go to the Bolsheviks

36. How did the Bolsheviks fare in the elections for the Constituent Assembly?

    A.   They received about one half of the vote
    B.   They received about three fourths of the vote
    C.   They received nearly 100 percent of the vote
    D.   They received about one quarter of the vote

37. Which best describes the response to the October Revolution in Moscow?

    A.   Unlike in Petrograd, the fighting went on in Moscow for nearly a week
    B.   There was almost no reaction in Moscow at all
    C.   A group of monarchists took control of the Kremlin
    D.   Resistance continued in Moscow for over six months

38. Who became the Russian foreign minister under Lenin?

    A.   Dzerzhinsky
    B.   Zinoviev
    C.   Trotsky
    D.   Stalin

REVIEW & RESOURCES

39. Immediately following the October Revolution, what was the state of the Bolsheviks' plans for managing the country?

    A. They had mapped out a highly detailed government structure in advance
    B. They improvised the government's structure as they went along
    C. They continued to use the same structure that the provisional government had created
    D. They invited the heads of socialist movements in Europe to help plan out Russia's future

40. Which organization was headed by Felix Dzerzhinsky?

    A. The Foreign Ministry
    B. The NKVD
    C. The Cheka
    D. The GOP

41. How many times did the Constituent Assembly meet?

    A. Once
    B. Twice
    C. Three times
    D. Four times

42. The Red Terror was a response to which event?

    A. The beginning of the Civil War
    B. A terrorist bombing in Petrograd
    C. An assassination attempt on Lenin
    D. The entrance of U.S. and British troops into Russia

43. In March 1918, the Russian capital was moved to

    A. Petrograd
    B. Moscow
    C. Kiev
    D. Minsk

44. In the Russian Civil War, who were the Bolsheviks' opponents?

    A. Monarchists
    B. Democrats
    C. Moderate socialists
    D. All of the above

45. Which representative body replaced the Constituent Assembly?

    A. The First Congress of Soviets
    B. The Second Congress of Soviets
    C. The Third Congress of Soviets
    D. The Executive Committee

46. The Kornilov affair can best be summed up as

    A. An attempted coup
    B. The inspiration for *Dr. Zhivago*
    C. A misunderstanding
    D. A terrorist plot

47. All of the following were groups involved in the Russian Civil War *except*

    A. The Reds
    B. The Whites
    C. The Blues
    D. The Greens

48. When did the Russian Civil War begin?

    A. Spring 1917
    B. Summer 1917
    C. Spring 1918
    D. Summer 1918

49. The Cheka was a forerunner of the

    A. Duma
    B. Petrograd Soviet
    C. Politburo
    D. KGB

50. The USSR finally collapsed in

    A. 1981
    B. 1989
    C. 1991
    D. 1993

Suggestions for Further Reading

FITZPATRICK, SHEILA. *The Russian Revolution*: New York, Oxford University Press. 2001.

GILBERT, MARTIN. *The First World War: A Complete History*. New York: Henry Holt, 1994.

PIPES, RICHARD. *A Concise History of the Russian Revolution*. New York:. Knopf, 1995.

TROTSKY, LEON. *The Russian Revolution: The Overthrow of Tzarism and the Triumph of the Soviets*. Edited by F. W. Dupee, from *The History of the Russian Revolution*. New York: Anchor Books, 1959.

ULAM, ADAM B. *The Bolsheviks: The Intellectual and Political History of the Triumph of Communism in Russia*: Cambridge, Massachusetts: Harvard University Press, 1998.

REVIEW & RESOURCES